Write Here, Write Now!

2022

A Poetic Auto-Ethnography of

the Near Northwest

Write Here, Write Now!

2022

A Poetic Auto-Ethnography of the Near Northwest

Edited by Captain Cam'Ron

Alicia Pattison, Advisor

ISBN: 978-1-7349589-7-3 (Print)
ISBN: 978-1-7349589-8-0 (Digital)

Foreword by KC Chan-Brose

The Write Here, Write Now! Social & Environmental Action Writing Camp (WHWN!) began as a dream to bring together writers with a passion for social justice in the Near Northwest & Riverside area. It quickly became something bigger. WHWN! is not just a week long camp, but a collaborative creative space for community youth and organizations to build real, tangible connections between each other and our world, across campus and community. Now in its third iteration, we asked how writing can help us to understand our connections to our natural world and to others in our communities.

This book aims to answer that question.

Over the course of two one-week long camps, area middle and high school students combined creativity with hands-on research, argumentation, and narrative writing to explore the natural world in their urban communities.

It has been my great pleasure to work alongside these writers over the past three years. I've seen many of them grow from year to year as they've discovered the generative energy of creating something with their hands. I've watched them enjoy the sensation of dirt on their palms, of the responsible stewardship of composting, and of moving their bodies with intent and kindness.

I've watched them learn and create and grow.

I am infinitely proud of the WHWN! Campers and I am so excited to see this book come to fruition so that you can be proud of them to.

I would like to offer a special thank you to Alicia Pattison, Cam'ron Phillips, Norman Minnick, and JP Hyde for contributing their time and energy to make this book a reality.

I would also like to thank Mark Latta and Angela Herrman for co-creating this camp and our undergraduate tutors, Grace Von Lehman, Valerie Fernandez, Yvette Clemons, and Simon Collins for learning alongside me as we've revised this camp over the years.

Thank you all for taking chances, making mistakes, and getting messy with me.

Finally, I want to thank our community partners at Groundwork Indy (Kay Hawthorne, Montell Hendricks, ElizabethWallin, Phylis Boyd, Ian Oehler, and Jasmine Tylor), Flanner House (Brandon Crosby, Ron Rice, and Nico Selm), and The Learning Tree (DeAmon Harges and Wildstyle Paschal).

Thank you for keeping our community beautiful, vibrant, and informed.

The Early Morning Lovers by Eva Alcaraz-Monje

Early morning blues come often. Looming over me, pushing sleep into my eyes. In front of me a lone boy, dazed in the fluorescent light. Slumped in a chair booth stuck to the side of the crumbly blue walls and sticky glass windows. I don't know what he was thinking but I do know he's empty. Lacking what I don't know, but it's obvious as a blaring siren. Then like a gift, a miracle, she appears. Entering the cafeteria, power walking across the room in ballet sweats. Mind full of racing thoughts. Billions of preoccupations, yet as she sees him, they all wash away. The effect on him is apparent, his head perking up. Life enters him and he sits up to welcome her. They hug for a still second, but to them it's probably an eternity. Caught up in themselves, not a care in the world. It's slightly disgusting for 8:30 in the morning, but it's sweet. It's loving, it's kind, and it's absolutely wonderful. No one is paying much attention to them, concentrating on their own small lives. Yet the love is there, it's alive, even in the dead hours of the morning.

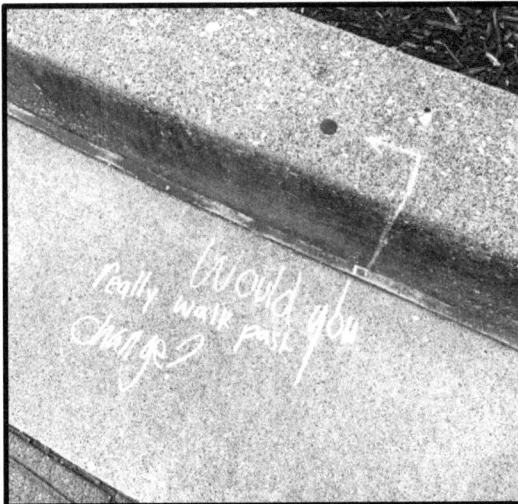

"Education is the passport of the future, For tomorrow belongs to those who prepare for it today." — Malcom X

Untitled by Kell Lowery

If a place that defines me gets damaged and threatened I would feel weird and out of place. One place that I would say I need is a connection with my mama because if it was to say I need my mother just in general with things. I would definitely say that's a place that I need in my heart.

One other place is if I lose my chill, like if somebody just makes me uncomfortable in situations it's like what can I do. I have social anxiety obstacles.

My grandmother's house I feel if I lose that place it would be hard for me because as I was raised we have been through a lot in that house. It would just be crazy and unorganized to me if I lose that part.

Our groundwork building was a lot we had to but we have lost it and it was a different kind of change. We lost our hill, plants etc. of what we had.

Threatened by Captain Cam'Ron

If a place that defines me was threatened
or destroyed, I would feel lost. For
example, if my ability to create
art was destroyed due to a life
life injury, I would be broken. I
love to draw, but if that is taken
away from me, I'm lost, I'm
broken, I'm annihilated. Making art
is my passion and if that is
taken away due to an injury
that can cause me never to use
my hands again would be the most
devastating thing that could
ever happen to me.

WHERE I'M FROM by Michael Doucette

I am from Dust
From Glucose and Oxygen
I am from the Intercostal
(Hot, Pretty, it smelled like salt)
I am from the Cherry Blossoms
Flowering and Beautiful
I'm from Perseverance, and Doing It Right The First Time
From Mom and Dad
I'm from the Love of each other and Kindness
From "Pain is weakness leaving the body" and "Losing is learning"
I'm from Christianity, and GOD FIRST
I'm from Pennsylvania and Nova Scotia
Corn and Wheat
From the Great Great Great grandfather who was in the Manhattan Project
The Olive skin of the Somrak side
In the safe
Anchoring me to home

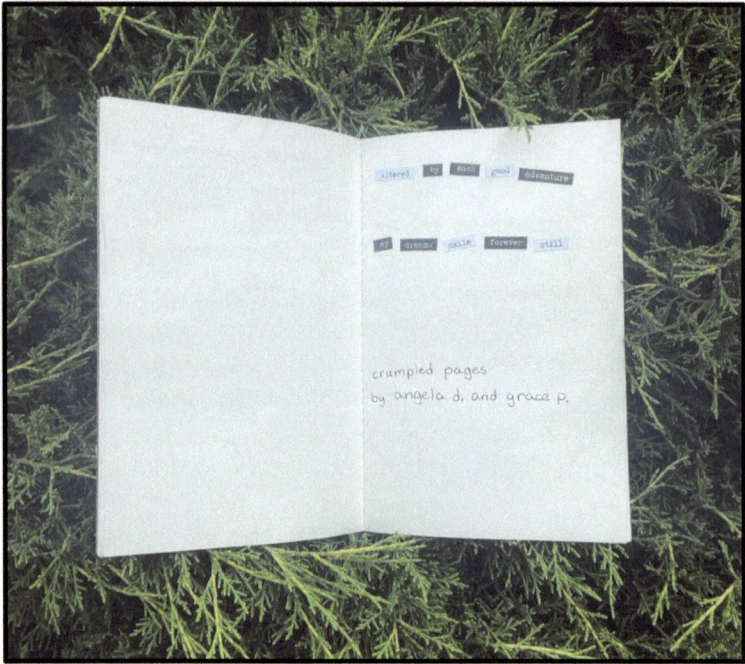

A poem by Angela and Grace

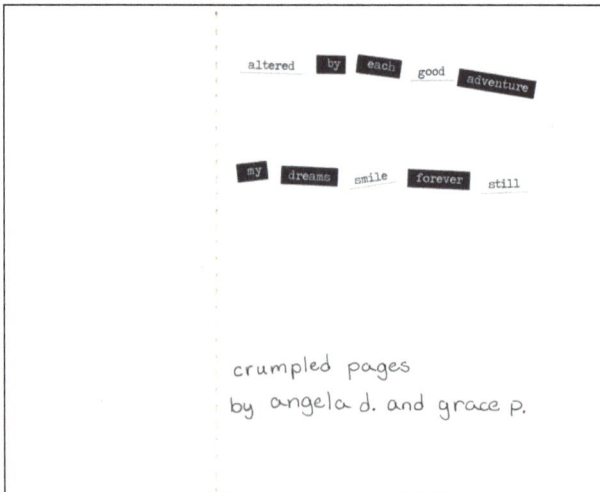

altered by each good adventure

my dreams smile forever still

crumpled pages
by angela d. and grace p.

The Hungry Turtle by Mark Boykin

Chapter 1

There was once a turtle sitting on a rock who was very hungry. He did a lot of thinking and was very wise. He was not very big or strong and he was not easy to please in the sense that he did not need much to be happy or satisfied with life. One day on his rock he saw a piece of paper blow by. He sat there observing and has been observing for 50 years now and not once has he seen this occur. At this moment he understood everything. He was now one with the universe.

Chapter 2

About 10 minutes later he felt a shift in the water. He knew what it was, it was Promethius. Prometheus never liked him and was obsessed with keeping our turtle friend away from his goal although what Promethius didn't know was that he was too late. Our turtle friend looked at Promethius and said I XXXX stand. Looked at our turtle friend, and saw balance and he felt fear and fled. Then a voice loud and quiet at the same time spoke up and said: "so you finally did it, you found the balance.

Chapter 3

Our turtle friend looks up to see his friend sitting on his head. The friend puts our turtle pull on the head and says congratulations to him. Our turtle friend looks up and sees our worst fears come true (of course he wasn't scared though) A gang of pirates come down and threw swords at our friends. To be continued.

"The Chess Players"

"Food is Fellowship"

"If more of us valued food and cheer and song above hoarded gold, it would be a much merrier world," — J.R.R Tolkien

The Dash by Grace Plumlee

I am walking through the large space, sidestepping the speckled, clean-cut rocks that seem to cover the entire yard. I stop in front of the familiar, graystone that's in the very corner of the space. I hear sobbing to my left, and look over. About 30 feet away. I see a woman with her hands in her face. A man beside her comforts her. My expression stays blank. I watch from afar as he pulls her to a car, tears still streaking down her face. I watch until the car is out of view, then I turn back to the stone in front of me. I drop to my knees, and I can feel the sun-warmed earth through the fabric of my jeans. My hand reaches out until I touch the warm stone. It's smooth. I trace over the letters that are carved into the rock, then I move down to the numbers below that. My hand stops at the dash between the two. What a funny concept "1902-1976" it reads. I stare at the small symbol between. Did that stand for her entire life? Did that stand for every heartbeat, every adventure, every experience of her life? Was that showing every smile and every tear? Was that showing every book read, every sentence written, every thought? Was that showing every dance that we did, laughing until our sides hurt and seeing which of us could embarrass ourselves with our "moves" first? Was that every breath, every frown, every dream? A dash didn't seem to convey the sheer vastness of her life, showing every experience she had or emotion she felt. A hundred dashes were in this graveyard each one representing the time between birth and death. But was that enough?

Mossy Embrace by Eva Alcaraz-Monje

Green moss
Soft, lush, thick.
Free flowing arms of seeds
scattering in the wind,
continuing the legacy.
Eternally stuck to wood,
to rock,
to water.
Growing along
with its environment.
Slowly, calmly.
Not in a hurry,
Just living and breathing
Spreading,
Wrapping more into its mossy embrace.
Sticking and holding it tight.
Not letting go.

This is called a Juneberry Tree. They are Native to North America, they are rarely and adjustable. This tree mainly grow in woodland areas. They are also native to all the States in US except Hawaii.

Photo by Mariah

"Embodiment"

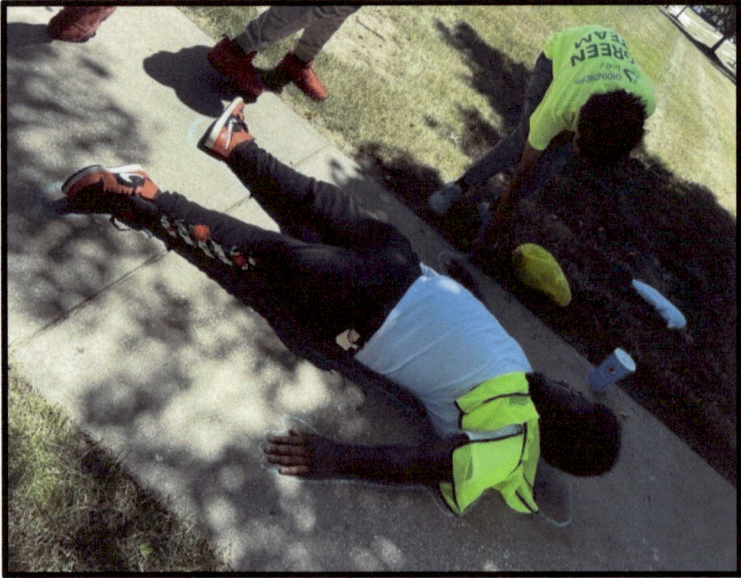

"Our future is our confidence and self-esteem," — Tupac Shakur

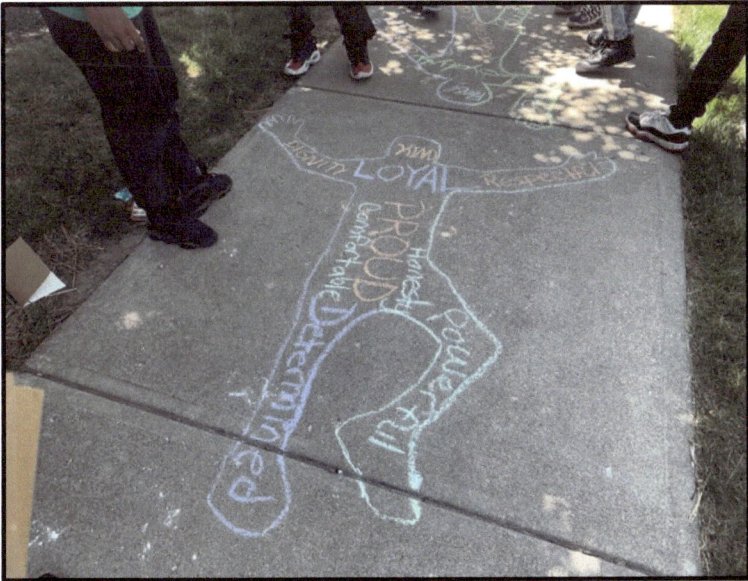

"We're all human at the end of the day, making mistakes.
But learn from them is key," — Kendrick Lamar

"Radishes Anyone?"

"I prefer"

I prefer dreads over waves
      cars over trucks
      Shoes over sandals
      movies over shows
      Football over basketball
      Dogs over cats
      Jordans over Nike
      summer over winter
      Miami over Nap
      MOM over anybody
      Water over Juice
      real food over snacks
      math over reading
      hardwood floors
      Rap music
      ethics

      — James Glass

              i prefer stay in the go out
              i prefer home food than out to eat
              i prefer anime than rerun tv shows
              i prefer ripped jeans
              i prefer dirt bikes
              i prefer chicken
              i prefer light skins
              i prefer football
              i prefer eating
              i prefer call of duty
              i prefer paintballing

              i rhinestone
              i prefer dogs
              i prefer tattoos
              i prefer money
              i prefer.

              — Taylor Smith

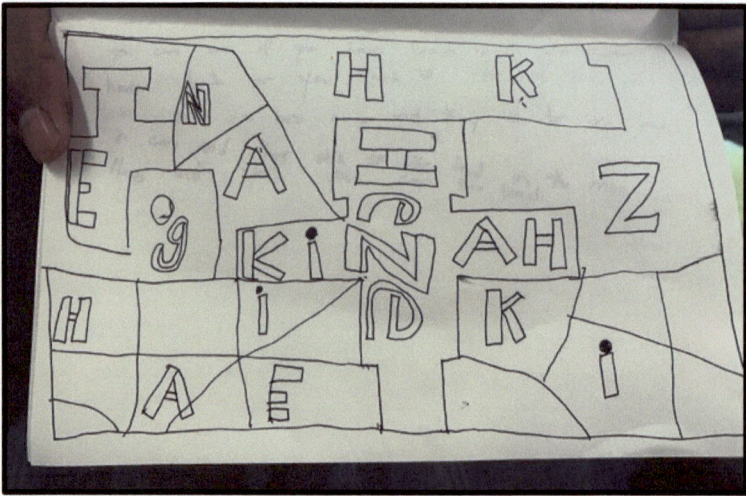

I prefer a lizard
I prefer Jerk 48 from Chicago
I prefer power movies
I prefer designer stuff
I prefer 2k
I prefer PS4
I prefer spring
I prefer Cali to Texas
I prefer night time
I prefer basketball
I prefer gym
I prefer outside
I prefer girls
I prefer track
I prefer walking
I prefer my dream
I prefer North Elsinore

— Hezekiah Jones

I prefer yellow
I prefer action movies
I prefer chicken wings
I prefer basketball
I prefer Jordans
I prefer fall
I prefer Atlanta
I prefer birds that talk
I prefer a BMW
I prefer lil durk
I prefer hotdogs with no ketchup
I prefer glasses
I prefer white socks
I prefer Ohio State
I prefer jazz
I prefer german shepard
I prefer black cinema
I prefer nature
I prefer nice hair
I prefer watermelon
I prefer loyalness
I prefer honesty

— Kell Lowery

I prefer polo g over lil Durk
I prefer dogs over cats
I prefer Juice over water
I prefer soul food over Chinese food
I prefer seafood over soul food
I prefer pink over purple
I prefer blue over pink
I prefer hoverboards over bikes
I prefer PS4 over PS5
I prefer nintendo over PS4
I prefer my afro puff over braids
I prefer oranges over apples
I prefer orange juice over apple juice
I prefer Kaylen over Kell
I prefer uncle Soso over uncle Darrell
I prefer no homework over homework
I prefer homemade food over restaurant food.
I prefer Hip HOP over JaZZ
I prefer videos over books
I prefer coloring over drawing
I prefer my mom over my dad
I prefer Laptops over computers
I prefer apple over android
I prefer strawberry over blueberry
I prefer gary indiana over nap

— Daneisha McIntosh

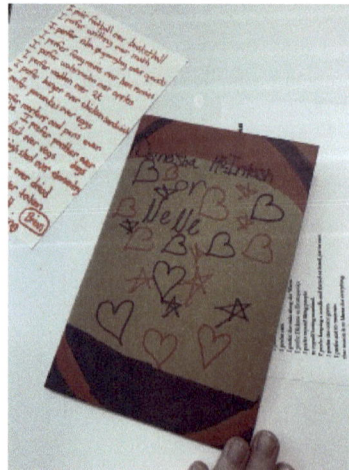

I prefer football over basketball
I prefer writing over math
I prefer NBA youngboy over quando
I prefer funny movies over home movies
I prefer watermelon over apples
I prefer madden over 2k
I prefer burger over chickens sandwich
I prefer pancakes over eggs
I prefer markers and pens over
Pencils. I prefer panther over
                              dogs
I prefer fruit over vegs
        I prefer high school over elementary
I prefer iphone over droid
I prefer single over taken
I prefer xbox over Ps4
I prefer car over walking

— Brian

                     I prefer dogs over cats
                     I prefer soul food over seafood
                     I prefer movies to TV
                     I prefer football to basketball
                     I prefer Jordan over Nike
                     I prefer carpet over wooden
                     I prefer madden over 2k
                     I prefer Tacos over Burritos
                     I prefer black over red
                     I prefer watermelon over grapes

                     — Black aka Blizzy

I Prefer

Rap, Dogs, Money, Iphones, Cook~food, Black, Baby's, Movies,
Math, Love, nice, Cakes, Dark

                     — Makyla Wray

I prefer

I prefer money
I prefer loyalty
I prefer something real
I prefer grinding all night
        instead of eating a meal

I prefer my freedom

I prefer living good
I prefer being Independent
        and not having nobody to lean on
I prefer being for the streets
I prefer being lonely before somebody
        try to play me
I prefer the 5

— Cory

"Jewelry as Storytelling"

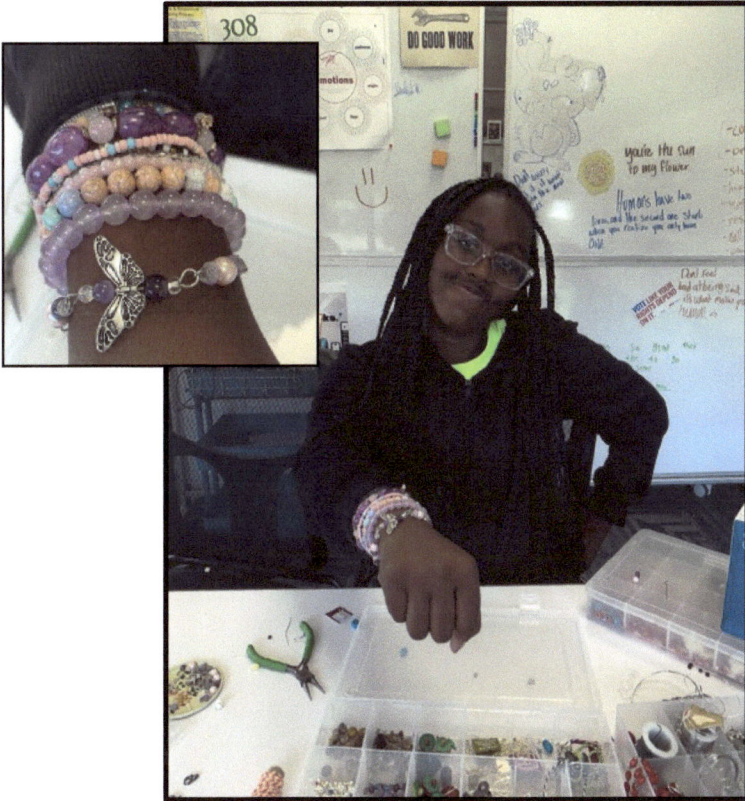

"All Things Purple"

"I think of God off if you walk by the color purple in a field some-
where and don't notice it." — Alice Walker

i prefer

the smell of old churches
warm blankets
to be in movement
and stay there
using too many adjectives
being loud
saying "i love you"-
even to friends
the simple cacophony of the country
bare feet
(minus the scattering of sticks)
vibrant colors
the resonant hum of an old tv
long hugs
trampolines
unabashed joy
softness, in all its forms
the imperfections of a record
and all the imperfections within myself

— inspired by Wisława Szymborska
— Yvette Clemons

I prefer yoga suits
bare arms in the chilly fall air, warmed by my own beating heart
breath of fire warming my belly, dirt under my fingernails, sweat on my brow
I prefer the smell of sage and the damp rotting wood
I prefer sunflowers, pregnant,
bowled over the weight of themselves as they try to keep pace with the sun
I prefer arms
big arms, strong arms, my husband's arms
and small arms, living necklaces
My children's wrapped around me

— KC Chan-Brose

"The Gift"

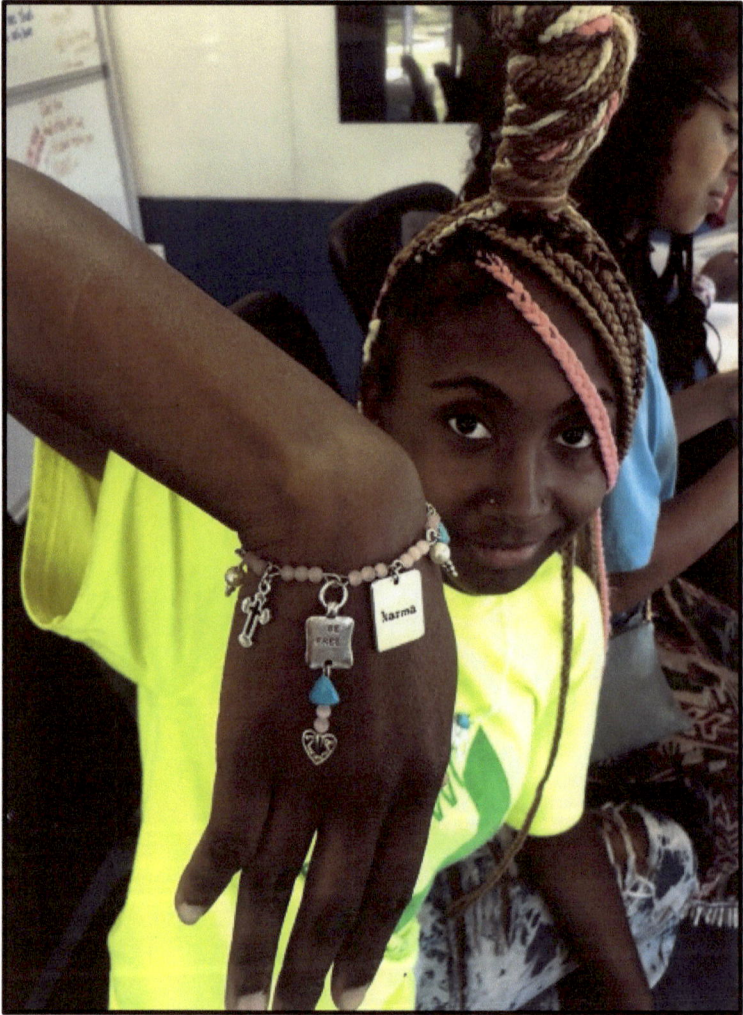

"Be You"

Untitled by Mia Banda

As I stand in the empty area, filled with tall trees and green grass, and small birds, flying above the trees and the mighty eagles, on the mountains. Seeking food.

The crowing of the black crowes, and the birds singing, really sets the mood.

I can see the prey of animals forming an alliance against the predators.

And the sound of the light rainfall hitting the leaves down below, filling the silence.

I close my eyes softly as the light drops of water fall on my head.

I breathe gently and slowly, not wanting to ruin this. I let out a small smile.

And then a small chuckle, then a laugh. I'm happy, I'm calm, I have no worries.

I have no idea how so many people can think that this beautiful nature is boring.

I hear very calming music, the kind you hear on ads, letting you know how sleep is important.

I don't know if it's real or if it's just my head being hypnotized by this euphoria, a hallucination?

It sounds beautiful, like the wind chimes on an old granny's porch.

I finally open my eyes to the gray clouds floating away. Revealing the clear blue sky.

And the bright, bright sun from way up high. Shines like a light on a diamond.

It blinds the sight of the human eye, but it is gorgeous to look at.

But I must enjoy this mother nature, this beauty, while I still have time.

Tree Village ©2022 by Joseph

Tree Village was once a hill age

It had all the green on the scene

their life would by better

Except for the weather

Torn Childs are wild

Hurricanes are their bane

The seeds destroyed in the weeds

After the storm

Back to the norm

Phew

The sun makes the leaves hum

Proud sprouts rise to their size

The End!

Untitled by Jack Thomas

So today I saw Many cars on our tour. And our project is about nature and I thought about the fuels and how to make the fuels less harmful to nature and so they don't kill animals. So to work on that we should invest in finding less harmful fuels. To help keep cars with engines and to not eliminate car enthusiasts like me. And how we do that is with biodiesel which can be made by mixing cooking oil with methoxide catalyst. And then there's others like ethanol fuel which is made from corn and other plants then there's also hydrogen fuel which you can mix with coal. And so if we don't do this then cars with engines will be gone and car enthusiasts will not exist anymore and cars with engines will just be tales we tell our children and grandchildren.

"Broquet"

The childhood I am from. By Eva Alcaraz-Monje

I am from the house in the middle.
The house in the condo complex,
locked with a green metal gate.
Always loud,
always rusty.
I am from linoleum floors,
peeling cabinets,
scribbled baby blue walls.
Always loud,
Always hot.
I am from lizards,
scaly travelers.
Big and small.
From swallowtail birds,
soaring in the skies.
From cockroaches,
resilient as a memory in my brain.
I am from late night Thai food,
Always mild curry
and white rice,
a distinct unmatchable delicious taste.
From free fried bananas,
loyal gifts from the chef.
Served with cool vanilla ice cream
rivaling the fresh hot sweets.
I am from that one Cuban café,
booths sticky with memories
of post ballet hot chocolate and cafecito.
Always freshly baked croquetas and empanadas,
cool tres leches,
warm empanadas.
I am from the Western Restaurant,
packed with love and grease.
Late afternoon after haircut dinners,
rushing to eat before 9.
Always perfect coleslaw and buttered toast,
rich char burgers,

fizzy sprite.
Messy coloring books,
scratched and torn,
A plethora of colored crayons.
I am from daily retellings,
interesting stories,
loving conversations,
noisy restaurants,
fond foods.
I am from that house in the middle.
Always home.

Nature by Captain Cam'Ron

Nature is my beauty
Like two lovers on a honeymoon
Nothing is as majetic
As the beauty of Nature

Some may like nature,
Other my not
But the sight of seeing the Beauty of flowers, trees and
Little Cabins in the forest makes me feel as if there
is a rainbow at the
End of this Journey.

Nature is a my beauty
No beauty is like nature,
Birds singing, Bees buzzing,
Earth would be nothing
Without Nature.

"The more clearly we can focus our attention on the wonders
and realities of the universe about us, the less taste we shall
have for destruction." — Rachel Carson

Photo by: Alicia Marie

Sit by Grace Plumlee

Sit.

When the sun throws her beams upon me, and when the moon breathes shade over me.

When the stillness of the world grabs a hold. And when the wind dances through me, sending ripples along my surface.

Sit.

And here I shall sit, perhaps waiting for the sun to pull me to the sky, to meet the clouds, or for rain to give to me.

Perhaps i will sit tomorrow, or till the end of forever.

No one shall care, or even notice.

"It is Dire Poverty Indeed when a man is so malnourished and fatigued that he will not stoop to pick up a penny."

— Annie Dillard

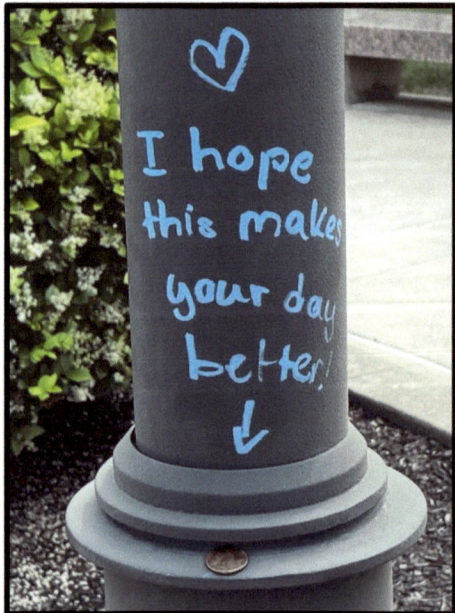

GALLERY PHOTOS

"Let us be good stewards of the earth we inherited. All of us have to share the earth's fragile ecosystems and precious resources, and each of us has a role to play in preserving them. If we are going to go on living together on this earth, we must all be responsible for it." — Kofi Annan

"Lunch Time"

"The Thinkers"

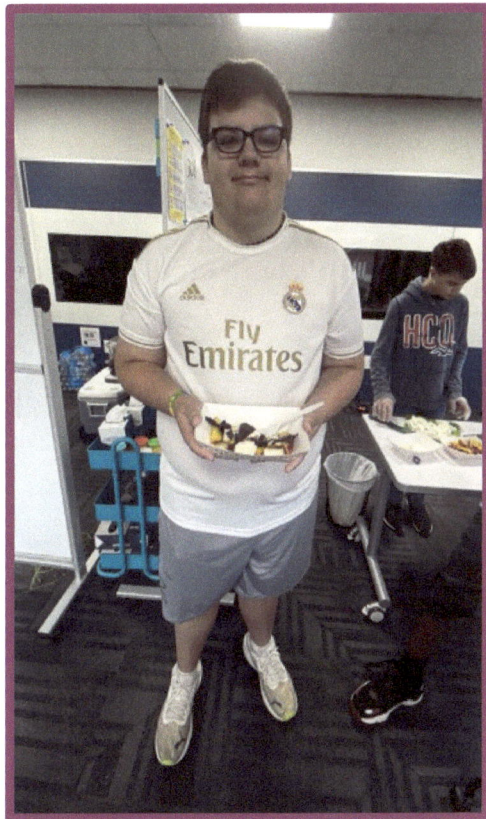

"Enjoying A Peach
Caprese Salad"

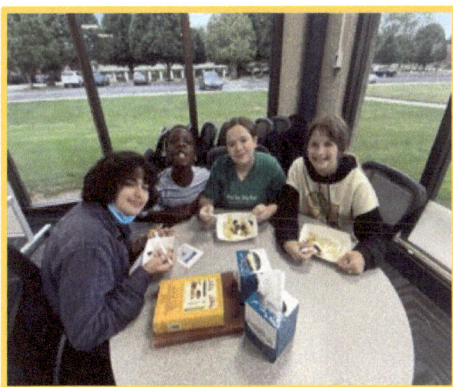

"I guess you can say that
I 'caprese'iate this salad"

"A Boy's Story"

"Unsure"

"Touring the EcoLab"

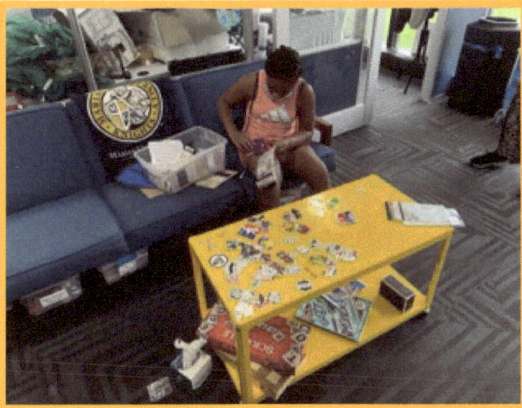

"Stick 'n' Fit"

"Two things people throughout history have in common are hatred and humour. I am proud that I have been able to use humour to lessen people's hatred."

— Richard Pryor

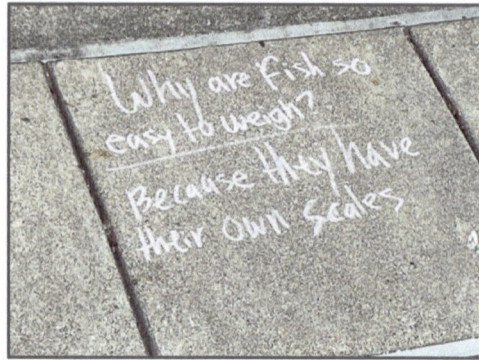

"Recipeople"

"Playing around in the Nature Center'

"Treedom"

"To be without trees would, in deed, in the most literal way, to be without our roots." — Richard Mabey

"All that glitters is not good" — Shakespeare

"Jewelry Jam"

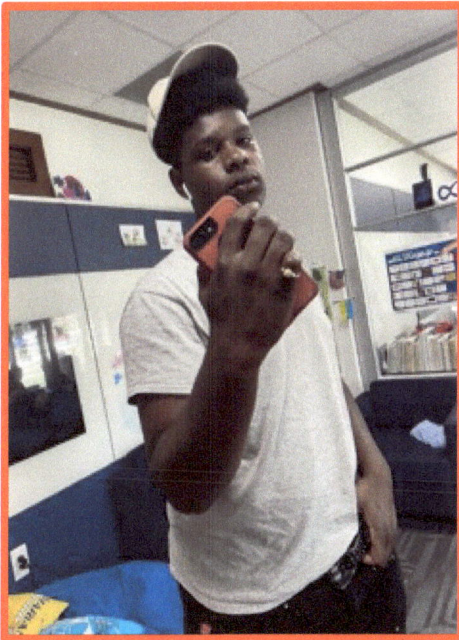

"Check Out My Bling
Bling Ring"

"A game of Hurling"

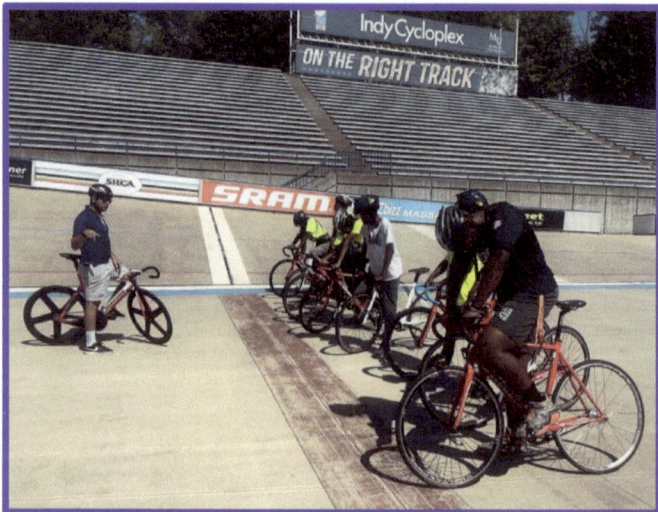

"Preparing to race at the Velodrome"

"The Race"

Flanner's Farm: Community Center

"History Of Our
Community"

"Karma's pot makes a cameo"

"Potting For Gold"

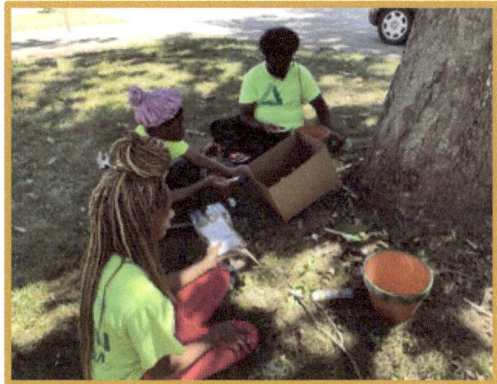

"We don't make mistakes, we just make happy accidents."
— Bob Ross

Write Here Write Now Crew

Groundwork's Indy Crew

Cover Artist's Statement

The Bird of Paradise by Captain Cam'Ron

The concept of this piece is to emphasize the feeling of being trapped.

Colored Pencil was the choice of this art piece due to the necessary action of blending and shading to get the best quality and detail of this piece of art.

The bird used in this piece is a female "Blue Bird of Paradise". They are native to New Guinea, an island in Australia. The males are known for their bizarre appearance. They have an orange fuzz and two long feather straps on their rear ends.. They are also known for their bizarre mating ritual, in which the males use their feathers to make a black face and start to vibrate and dance.

The monochromatic background of the piece is used to explain the unexplored, how the way it feels to be trapped in the same environment, the same routine, and the same setting. The box that separates the monochromatic to the technicolor is to show the cage that is blocking the bird. The bird wants to see a new environment and explore new territories, but can't due to its characteristics and inhabitants.

www.ingramcontent.com/pod-product-compliance
Lightning Source LLC
Chambersburg PA
CBHW040037100420
42734CB00035B/82